AMELIA EARHART
QUEEN OF THE SKY

Mark Mallory

New York

Published in 2009 by The Rosen Publishing Group, Inc.
29 East 21st Street, New York, NY 10010

Book Design: Michael J. Flynn

Photo Credits: Cover, pp. 5, 12 © Getty Images News/Getty Images; p. 6 (glider) © Henry Guttmann/
Hulton Archive/Getty Images; p. 6 (Wright bi-plane) © Central Press/Hulton Archive/Getty Images;
p. 6 (hot-air balloons) © Nathan Shahan/Shutterstock; p. 9 © Richard Sargeant/Shutterstock;
p. 10 © Topical Press Agency/Hulton Archive/Getty Images.

ISBN: 978-1-4358-0053-3
6-pack ISBN: 978-1-4358-0054-0

Manufactured in the United States of America

CONTENTS

AMELIA EARHART

Amelia Earhart was a famous **pilot**.

She was born in 1897.

Amelia liked to see and do new things.

She enjoyed watching planes do tricks.

When she was in her 20s, she had
her first ride in an airplane.

Amelia decided she wanted to fly.

She took **lessons** and quickly learned.

This picture shows Amelia Earhart getting ready to fly. ▶

MACHINES THAT FLY

People have always wanted to fly.

They went up in hot-air balloons.

People also went up in **gliders**.

Gliders use forces of air to fly.

In 1909, the Wright brothers built
an airplane with an **engine**.
Airplanes with engines could stay
in the air longer than gliders.

 **Hot-air balloons, gliders, and the Wright brothers'
airplane were some early methods of flight.**

RECORD SETTER

In Amelia's time, very few women flew airplanes.

She set many flying records.

She flew higher than other women pilots.

She also set new speed and **distance** records.

In 1932, Amelia became the first woman pilot

to fly across a **continent**.

Amelia Earhart's airplane, the *Canary*, had two pairs
of wings, just as this airplane does.

Amelia Earhart

A crowd welcomed Amelia after she finished her flight across the Atlantic Ocean.

10

ACROSS AN OCEAN!

Amelia Earhart wanted to set another record.
In 1932, she became the first woman
to fly across the **Atlantic Ocean** alone.
She didn't let bad weather or problems
with her airplane stop her.
Amelia Earhart was the Queen of the Sky!

AMELIA EARHART
QUEEN OF THE SKY

- flew higher than other women pilots
- first woman to fly alone across the Atlantic Ocean
- flew faster than other women pilots
- first woman to fly across a continent

AROUND THE WORLD

Amelia wanted to fly around the world.
She wasn't the first to do this, but the path
she planned to follow would make
her flight the longest.
In 1937, she began the flight.
It was the last flight she would ever take.

 In this picture, Amelia is standing in front of one of her airplanes.

LOST!

Amelia ran into many problems.

Heavy rains, broken plane parts,

and illness cost her time.

Radio calls from Amelia's plane stopped

as she was flying over the **Pacific Ocean**.

Amelia and her plane were never seen again!

IMPORTANT HAPPENINGS IN AMELIA'S LIFE

- 1897   Amelia Earhart is born.

- 1909   Wright brothers build and fly an airplane with an engine.

- 1930   Amelia sets the women's world flying speed record.

- 1932   Amelia flies alone across the Atlantic Ocean. She is also the first woman to fly across a continent.

- 1937   Amelia is lost over the Pacific Ocean.

GLOSSARY

Atlantic Ocean (uht-LAN-tihk OH-shun) The body of water between the Americas and Europe and Africa.

continent (KAHN-tuh-nuhnt) One of the seven great bodies of land on Earth.

distance (DIHS-tuhns) Length.

engine (EHN-juhn) A machine that changes electricity into movement.

glider (GLY-duhr) An airplane without an engine.

lesson (LEH-suhn) Something that helps you learn.

Pacific Ocean (puh-SIH-fihk OH-shun) The body of water between the Americas and Asia and Australia.

pilot (PY-luht) A person who flies an airplane.

INDEX